The Fate of Rural Hell

BENEDICT ANDERSON

The Fate of Rural Hell

Asceticism and Desire in Buddhist Thailand

LONDON NEW YORK CALCUTTA

Seagull Books, 2016

Text © Benedict Anderson, 2012
Images © Individual photographers
'In Hell' © Marina Warner, 2012
Letters © respective authors/estates

First published by Seagull Books in 2012

ISBN 978 0 8574 2 402 0

British Library Cataloguing-in-Publication Data
A catalogue record for this book is available
from the British Library

Designed by Bishan Samaddar, Seagull Books, Calcutta, India
Printed and bound by Hyam Enterprises, Calcutta, India

Contents

Acknowledgements

The rough English draft of this book was stimulated by the notes taken in 1999 by my former student (now a prominent public intellectual), Mukhom Wongthes, when she, Adadol (May) Ingawanij and I went to Wat Phai Rong Wua. Added to, corrected, re-photographed and re-contextualized by Chaisiri Jiwarangsan, Apichatpong Weerasetakul and Sitanan Raweerid, it was translated into Thai by Adadol and, aimed at a Thai readership, was eventually published in Thailand's leading critical intellectual journal *Aan*, superbly edited by Ida Aroonwong. For this re-Anglicization, aimed at a global readership, I owe everything to Naveen Kishore and his colleagues at Seagull Books. This version has been partly added to and deepened by Kamala Tiyavanich, who explained to me many things about Thai Buddhism as well as its Indian origins; my student Lawrence Chua and Professor Pasuk Phongpaichit for introducing m to the economic and aesthetic history of ferroconcrete in Thailand; Siriwut Buncheun, whose skill in Japanese allowed me to understand the strange Japanese guidebook to hells in Thailand and who took me to Wat Phradeuchadom; and, finally, my long-time Indonesian assistant Eduward Manik, who is digitalizing my photographs taken in East and South East Asia over the past 50 years and has given this archive the highest possible technical quality. My gratitude to all these wonderful friends is unlimited.

Strange Ghosts

I first visited Wat Phai Rong Wua in 1975. In those distant, happy, briefly democratic days,[1] one could not reach it by road but only by taking a boat up the Ta Chin River and then veering into a tributary which ended up as a short, new canal alongside the extensive grounds of the *wat* (Buddhist temple). Some friends had said with cheerful Bangkok condescension: 'It's in the middle of nowhere but it's really worth a look!' They described a vast complex of buildings, created by Luang Phor Khom (venerable monk named Khom), a charismatic abbot with a strong following in the Bangkok moneyed elite, to show Buddhism in Siam in a new, global light. Unlike the usual Thai *wat*, exclusive

[1] On 14 October 1973, huge protesting crowds in Bangkok overthrew the 15-year military dictatorship of Field Marshal Sarit Thanarat and his epigones. Free elections produced a parliament in which, for the only time in modern Thai history, socialist and left-leaning liberals were elected. On 6 October 1976, a bloody military coup took place and many students and activists were murdered, imprisoned or driven to flee to the Thai Communist Party's guerrilla forces in the maquis.

in spirit, Wat Phai Rong Wua was, they said, ecumenical, centred on Theravada Buddhism but offering space for Mahayana Buddhist and Brahmanic Hindu shrines, statues and images—and even, at the margins, emblems of Confucian Taoism, Islam and Christianity. This outlook seems similar to what today Thai call the *sakon* (international) ambition, which includes a demand for world recognition and offers a reciprocal recognition of the world.

My first reaction was simply astonishment at the sheer scale of the *wat,* and its spick-and-span look. The second was the strange feeling that I had wandered into a sort of religious Disneyland. A gigantic simulacrum of a Hindu temple in India was just that. There were no devotees and the interior decoration was perfunctory. It looked like a set for a historical film. What were two large concrete camels, painted red, doing at one of the main gates? No one but a few curious tourists had any visible interest in the Chinese shrine. Even stranger was Luang Phor Khom's personal museum which included, side by side, an upright human skeleton in a glass cabinet and a life-size replica of

IMAGE 1 (*previous pages*) Picture of the little pier and the big canal leading to Wat Phai Rong Wua (1975). *All photographs in this volume are by the author unless otherwise mentioned.*

IMAGE 2 (*facing page*) A Mahayana Buddha among various Hinayana ones: an instance of the *sakon* ambition (2006).

IMAGE 3 One of the outside gates to Wat Phai Rong Wua. The camel is a sign of Islam gathered under the wing of Buddhism (2006).

IMAGE 4 Replica of a Hindu temple, yet another sign of internationalism (2006).

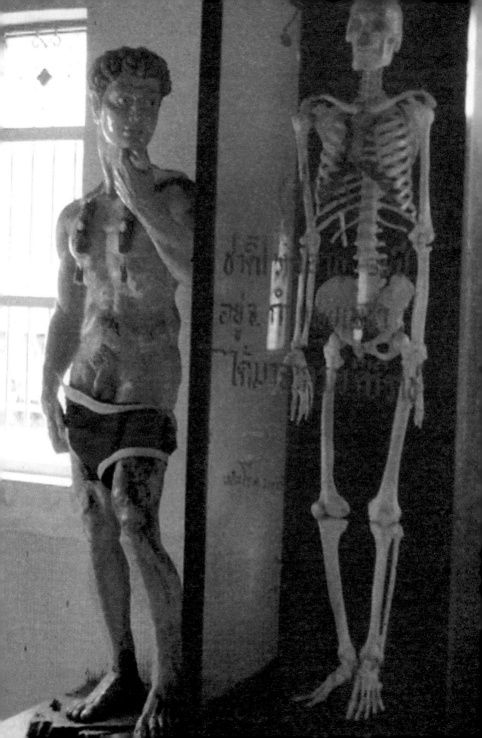

Michelangelo's gigantic nude *David* wearing fashionable red underpants from the top of which poked part of a swollen, unflorentine penis. The initial Disney effect was, however, undercut by a general emptiness: only a few monks, no novices, no nuns and very few lay persons. For whom was the *wat*—in this (then) hard-to-access corner of rural Suphanburi—intended? I had no idea.

I did not go back to Wat Phai Rong Wua till the 1990s, not long after the death of Luang Phor Khom in January that year, at the age of 88, after 68 years as a monk. General Suchinda Krapayoon's disastrous coup as only a year away in the future. The place had started to decay. Quickly made cement statues were crumbling, paint was flaking off everywhere, the vast open spaces were littered with used plastic bags and other wrappings, empty bottles, bits of newspaper, fragments of flip-flop slippers and so on. Only a handful of listless vendors could be seen. The whole place seemed desolate. Later it occurred to me that Luang Phor Khom had probably never calculated the maintenance cost of his colossal *wat* and, even more probably, was not capable of raising lots of money in his final days— perhaps because of his age, perhaps because the Siam of

IMAGE 5 (*facing page*) The human skeleton stands next to a micro-version of Michelangelo's *David* (1975).

the 1970s was gone for ever. Big money had begun to come into the province but it was going to the city of Suphanburi, home to Banharn Silpa-archa, the powerful, ambitious Sino-Thai politician who eventually became prime minister (1995–96) and whose lavish pork-barrel projects were making people joke that the city's name should be changed to Banharnburi.[2]

Walking round in a slightly gloomy mood, my eye was caught by some noisy activity in a part of the complex that I had previously overlooked. A cheerful, tough-looking guy, heavily tattooed, was busy shaping a new statue to join the dozens of others representing evildoers being ferociously punished in 'hell'. We chatted briefly and I asked him why the *wat* was so empty. He said something that stuck in my memory: 'This part of the *wat*, at least, always has plenty of visitors.' 'Who comes?' 'Mostly parents and school-teachers bringing youngsters to see what will happen to them if they turn bad.' What I noticed, but did not dare ask about, was that all but two of the tormented 'sinners' were stark naked, and that the males among them were given unusually large and sometimes swollen penises.

---

2 See the fine monograph by Yoshinori Nishizaki: *Political Authority and Provincial Identity in Thailand: The Making of Banharn-buri* (Ithaca, NY: Cornell University Southeast Asia Program, 2011).

Hell was still growing, but monumental construction seemed to have long ground to a halt.

Almost 10 years after that I went back again with the idea of writing something about the *wat*, especially its unusual Narokphum (hell). My friends Mukhom Wongthes and May Ingawanij kindly went along to guide and help me. The *wat* itself seemed to have recovered a bit: some repainting, extensive tidying up, many more Buddha statues—both Hinayana and Mahayana—and quite a lot of monks. But still no novices or nuns. Narokphum seemed to be growing but very slowly.

It was at this juncture that the three of us started to think about investigating this rural hell within its local and wider contexts. The first puzzle was why all of Narokphum's horribly tortured victims had 'captions' inscribed on their bodies in which they were referred to as *praed* (hungry ghosts). In everyday speech of the street sort, one can often hear people being cheerfully greeted as *ai praed*. *Ai* is a colloquial term of address to males, and can express either contempt or close friendship in the same cheerful tonality as *ai ha* (*ha* is literally 'small pox' or 'plague'), *ai hia* (*hia* is a large, water monitor lizard that feeds on carrion) and *ai krador* (*krador* means 'penis'). Nothing particularly terrible. The general lay idea is that the *praed* are ghosts of people whose sins were minor. Their sad and bleak afterworld is still close to the human world and they meet with no torturers. The figure for their condition is a spirit ravaged by perpetual hunger, especially for blood and pus, but with a mouth the size of a pinhole.

We decided to tackle the puzzle by making an inventory of all the captions. What sins would the list encompass? Could the list tell us something about the attitudes and intentions of the creators of Narokphum? Would it also have *sakon* characteristics? One thing was obvious after a single count: there was no great gender discrimination. The male *praed* outnumbered their female counterparts but not in a conspicuous manner.

Mukhom copied all the inscriptions into her notebook and organized them, in a simple ad hoc manner, into the following categories:

a. Wives and Husbands (19 statues): She—nagged her husband; only cared about herself; ran away from her husband in search of fun; slandered her husband to other people; forced him to cook rice; liked to curse her husband; quarrelled with another woman over a man; stayed up till her husband came home late at night; slandered her parents-in-law; had no morals and took lovers.

IMAGE 6 *(facing page)* A female *praed*. Her 'tag' says she liked to stay up late for her man (2006).

He—ran away from his wife to have fun; liked to swear at his wife and children; enjoyed beating his wife; quarrelled with another man over a woman; married a minor; didn't love his wife and children; had affairs; seduced women and enjoyed hurting them.

b. Parents and Children (13 statues): Parents— favoured some children over the others; (father) didn't love the children and their mother; (mother) had an abortion (twice); (parents) were unfair. Children—lied to their parents and to the monks; didn't take care of their parents in old age; refused to *wai* (humble greeting) to their parents; were disobedient; threatened to extort money from their mothers; cursed and beat their parents; didn't love their parents.

c. Offences against Monks (12 statues): He—ruined religion; cut off the heads of Buddha images; cursed monks; destroyed *wat* property; embezzled *wat* money; ate before the monks did; stole wood from the *wat*; stole fruit from the *wat*; ate fish from the *wat* and stole turtles from the *wat*. She—liked to chat up or flirt with monks; and liked to meet lovers on the *wat*'s premises.

IMAGE 7 *(facing page)* Male *praed* being tortured (2006).

IMAGE **8** Female *praed*. She had had an abortion (2006).

IMAGE 9 Female *praed*. She liked to flirt with monks (2006).

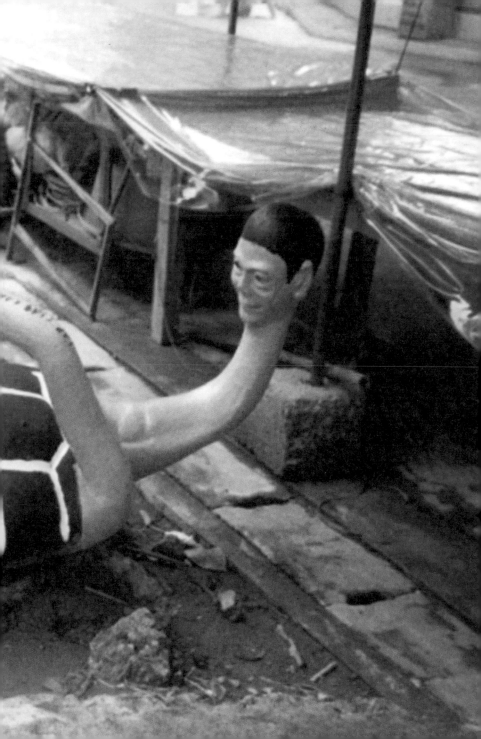

d. Offences against Animals (9 statues): People (both genders) who liked to torture animals; killed pigs; killed birds; killed ducks; liked to hurt chickens; enjoyed spearing frogs; tormented horses; and castrated and rustled carabaos. (All these *praed* have human bodies but their heads are those of the animals they abused or slaughtered.)

e. Miscellaneous Bad Behaviour (55 statues): Speech—slandered; shouted abuse; enjoyed lying to and deceiving others; spread malicious gossip; swore at benefactors. Actions/character—was selfish; liked to get drunk and not work; told lies and cheated; was lazy; was hypocritical and two-faced; was lewd; refused to admit to misbehaviour; liked obscene acts; put on a pious face but was really nasty inside; was miserly and did not pay back loans; liked to play cards for money; liked to cast fishing nets; enjoyed boxing; had no ethical values; devoured gifts meant for others; had itchy fingers; liked to cheat people; enjoyed pilfering; liked to be a

IMAGE 10 (*previous pages*) Male *praed*. He liked to kill turtles in the *wat* (2006).

IMAGE 11 (*facing page*) Female *praed*. She used to sell drugs (2006).

IMAGE 12 (*following pages*) Male *praed*. He had been a drunkard in his old age (2009). *Photograph by Chaisiri Jiwarangsan.*

peeping Tom; liked to go out to drink or pursue women; liked to gamble on boxing; was a thief; liked to drink; sold goods using crooked scales; liked to steal; (he) had no fear of *baap* (sin); (she) was not ashamed of *baap*; liked to kidnap children and sell them; enjoyed picking pockets; demanded a share in others' Buddhist merit; was a 'dirty old man'; was a petty thief; stole bananas; cheated people about land; illegally felled trees; robbed and killed; killed benefactors; strangled people; committed suicide; embezzled public money; was possessed by spirits; became addicted to heroin; liked to sell drugs; became addicted to drugs; went crazy over crack or smoked marijuana.

Mukhom's rough-and-ready classification underlines some interesting things. At least as far as Narokphum was concerned, my Bangkok friends of the 1970s were plainly mistaken. Its inhabitants are exclusively Thai who had violated the rules of Theravada Buddhism. No white 'Christian' Westerners, no bearded Muslims and no dark-skinned Hindus. Not a trace of anything at the *radap sakon* (international level). Perhaps not even at the national level. The moral axis of Narokphum lies between the monkhood

IMAGE 13 *(facing page)* Male *praed*. He used to smoke marijuana (2006).

IMAGE 14 To the left, female *praed* who was cruel to her man. In front, male *praed* who was a crack addict. to the right, male *praed* who liked to torture mice (2009). *Photograph by Apichatpong Weerasetakul.*

IMAGE 15 Male *praed*. He liked to torture frogs in the *wat* (2006).

and working rural families. If parents are good (to each other, to their relatives, their elders and their children) and if the privileges of the monks are respected, a sound (rural) social order should exist. The sins depicted are mostly understood as both rural and traditional—murder, lying, stealing, adultery, domestic violence, slander, disrespect for the elderly, small-scale cheating, favoritism, selfishness and so on. It is only in the case of drugs that we can detect something 'contemporary' and/or 'global'. The people we do *not* see being tortured are a curious lot: no rapists, no prostitutes (female or male), no political criminals, no committers of *lèse majesté*, no homosexuals or *krathoey* (transvestites), no police abusing state power, no communists, no professional hitmen, no capitalists and, naturally, no bad monks. The *wat* frequently appears as a victim of evildoing. Not only is its property the chief target of thieves—money, fish, trees, turtles, etc.—but the monks' honour is also under attack from female flirting, male insolence, even hostility. Both sexes also use the temple grounds for illicit sex at night. The captions relating to the *wat* also show some of the limits on the universalism of Buddhism in its rural Suphanburi surroundings. Killing fish in general is not condemned, only killing fish in the *wat*'s ponds. Sex between unmarried people in general is

IMAGE 16 (*facing page*) Female and male *praed*. They liked to look for sex in the *wat* (2006).

IMAGE 17 (*facing page*) Male *praed*. He used to embezzle public money (2006).

IMAGE 18 (*this page top*) Male *praed*. He was lazy (2009). *Photograph by Chaisiri Jiwarangsan.*

IMAGE 19 (*this page bottom*) Male *praed*. He liked to lie to and cheat people (2006).

not punishable, only when they do it in the *wat*. In the same way, one notices that the only people who are tortured for their behaviour to animals are those who kill or torment edible domestic animals—fish, ducks, pigs, carabao, turtles and, at the limit, horses. Not a word about dogs or cats, let alone wild animals (snakes, crocodiles, scorpions, etc.)—except maybe edible wild deer (see p. 78). All very local.

What Mukhom's orderly inventory necessarily hides from view is Narokphum's internal chaos. There is absolutely no hierarchy of punishments whose severity is coordinated with the gravity of the *baap*. The wife who forces her husband to cook rice at home is tortured just as horribly as the murderer. The same is true of the wretched addict and his criminal drugdealer, the woman who chats up monks and the son who extorts money from his mother with threats of violence. The absence of order (compare Catholicism's seven circles of Hell) is also clear from the sites of the statues themselves which are scattered about, higgledy-piggledy: the turtle-stealer, the armed robber, a cheeky child and the woman who has had an abortion are placidly located side by side.

Discussing our visit with Mukhom and May, I proposed an explanation of this chaos: market forces. If most of the statues were 'commissioned' by locals or visitors—say a mother, worried that her teenage son might be becoming a drug addict or that her boy-crazy daughter might get pregnant and want an abortion, could perhaps commission torture statues of an addict or woman who'd had an abortion to which she could bring her children— then the statues would be tailored to different kinds of customers.[3] There was no reason to be orderly or to calibrate punishments. Every client would want his or her statue to be as frightening as possible. Sheer consumer demand.

---

3 A small digression. My companions were somewhat puzzled by the seeming isomorphism at this *wat* between Narokphum and the *praed*. They said that Narok or Narokphum is a huge, separate 'world' of its own, divided into different parts. But they thought that the *praed* were very much part of the human world. They suffer in themselves and do not need to be tortured by *phayayom* (cruel agents of Yama, God of the Underworld). Interviewed by my friend Chaisiri Wijarangsan in February 2009, Suchart aka Ai Lek, the chief sculptor of this Narokphum, said in a rather confused, or confusing, way that Luang Phor Khom wanted his hell to be inhabited only by human beings—without any non-human evil spirits.

Luang Phor Khom and His Times

My explanation was wrong. During recent interviews with monks at the *wat*, they insisted that every single statue was personally 'ordered' by Luang Phor Khom. If they were telling the truth, then a serious explanation might emerge from a closer look at the abbot's life. In any case, the abbot's biography would have to be the key to grasping the psychic turbulence of Wat Phai Rong Wua as a whole. In the account that follows, I rely on the *wat*'s official brochure, two academic theses and two long interviews with monks.[4]

---

4 The two theses are: Phramaha Suthep Phiwpheuad, 'Phonkrathop sangkhom lae watthanatham khong kanthongthiauw thi mi tor wat lae chumchon: syksa chapho koroni Wat Phai Rong Wua, Tambon Bang Ta Then, Ampheur Song Phi Nong, Jangwad Suphanburi' (The Social and Cultural Impact of Tourism on Buddhist Temples and Local Communities: A Case Study of Wat Phai Rong Wua, Sub-District of Bang Ta Then, District of Song Phi Nong, Province of Suphanburi) (MA thesis, Thammasat University, 2002); Sanoh Thianthong, 'Wicha wikhro lak Putthathamma thi prakot yu nai Putthasilpa; syksa chapho koroni Phrakru Uphaiphadathorn (Luang Phor Khom), Wat Phai Rong Wua, Jangwad Suphanburi' (Analytical Study of Basic Buddhist Teachings as They Appear in Buddhist Art: A Case Study of Phrakru Uphaiphadathorn (Luang Phor Khom), Wat Phai Rong Wua, Province of Suphanburi) (MA

The strange man who became Luang Phor Khom was born on 11 May 1902 in the hamlet of Ban Phai Do in the Takhian sub-district Takhian, Song Phi Nong district, Suphanburi province.[5] In those days it was a very isolated, marshy, thinly populated but fertile place in a region where everyone spoke the local dialect. In his later years Luang Phor Khom said:

> I remember when Wat Phai Wong Wua was built. It was in an unlikely place, situated in an isolated rice field. Houses were scattered far apart. I had to visit so many homes on my early rounds to receive food alms that by the time I got back to the *wat* the sun was already high in the sky.[6]

His childhood was thus spent during the final years of Rama V's rule (1868–1910) and the first years of that of Rama VI (1910–25). He was the fifth son (probably the

---

thesis, Mahachulalongkornradjavidyalaya University, 2005). These sources will hereafter be abbreviated as PSP and ST respectively. The official brochure is henceforth referred to as OB. All quotations from these sources appear in my translation.

5 The date can be read symbolically: that same year the modernizing, absolutizing King Rama V decreed the creation of a centralized Sangha bureaucracy led by his brother Prince Wachirayan. The idea was to standardize a single form of Buddhist doctrine and practice, using the Bangkok version of Thai, and impose this on a country that had many local traditions and used many different dialects and languages. For the first time in Thai history, monkhood was put firmly under state control.

6 PSP, p. 52.

'baby' boy), with seven siblings, of a farming couple known as Mr Chang and Mrs Prem Kaewsuwat.[7] Pao, as they named him, was a delicate, sickly child; so, although he was eager to help with farming jobs, his worried parents decided to send him to the only school available, in nearby Wat Bang Saam. He took to study like a duck to water (the rest of his family was probably illiterate), and his robed teacher was sufficiently impressed to start training him to read and write in Khom, i.e. Old Cambodian. Pao's progress led his envious classmates to say that he was not a true Thai but a Khom and to give him the sarcastic *cheu len* (nickname) 'Ai Khom' which stuck to him for the rest of his life. As was common at that time, he lived at the *wat* (returning home only once in a while) and absorbed its discipline and routines.[8] After completing his basic lessons by the age of nine he was sent, with the help of a local monk, for further study at an elementary 'national school'—recently installed in Bangkok's famous Wat Sraket—where he first encountered a state-controlled modern style of primary education. Three years later (1914), after completing third grade, he returned home to help his parents.[9] The brochure describes him as a solitary

---

7 OB, *n.d.*; ST, p. 124
8 OB, *n.d.*
9 Ibid.; ST, p. 124.

teenager who did not care for the *he-ha-kan* (hanging out, drinking together, telling dirty jokes, hunting women) culture of rural males (but did this culture exist in, say, 1915?). There is no sign that he joined other boys in pursuing girls of the same age. When he was old enough, he was happy to be ordained on 7 May 1922 at Wat Bang Saam.

In 1926, a *thudong* (forest monk) called Phra Rung settled for a while in Luang Phor Khom's home hamlet. While still a layman, Phra Rung had been a friend of a villager called Mr Sorn.[10] A local 'big man', Mr Chu, donated 20 *rai* (32,000 square metres) of his land to Phra Rung in order to encourage him to settle permanently and build a *wat*. But two years later the restless forest monk took to the road again. A delegation was sent to the abbot of Wat Bang Saam to ask for a replacement. The abbot agreed to

---

10 Forest monks reject settling permanently in *wat* and lead wandering, often solitary, lives in deep forests, caves or mountain grottos. They concentrate on meditation rather than temple rites, practice herbal medicine and astrology and, unlike sedentary *wat* monks, have little regard for the 'academic' study of written Buddhist texts. In rural areas, especially in North and Northeast Siam, they are deeply revered for their austerity and selflessness. A marvellous description of forest monks can be found in Kamala Tiyavanich, *Forest Recollections: Wandering Monks in Twentieth-Century Thailand* (Honolulu: University of Hawaii Press, 1997). Needless to say, the post-1902 Sangha bureaucracy scorned and feared such monks.

send two monks: the new abbot, Phra Khauw, and, as his assistant, little 'Phra' Khom. Much later in his life, Phra Khom described the scene:

> When I came to stay at Wat Phai Rong Wua, building had only started about a year earlier. Actually, it was not really a *wat* but just quarters for two or three monks. There was also an open pavilion with mud floors and a thatched roof, used for merit-making events, as well as a small prayer-hall and a tiny pond. If the pond ran dry, we had to walk about one kilometre to fetch water from the Ta Chin River.[11]

Phra Khom stayed only briefly, since he wanted to acquire the necessary academic qualifications to create a little school and make the newborn *wat* an effective propagator of Buddhism. He moved to the town of Suphanburi and, over the next six years (1929–34) of schooling, successfully passed examinations at Wat Pratuu Saan for Dharma scholars—classes three, two and one. Meanwhile, the incipient *wat* had fallen on hard times: Phra Khauw disrobed after five years, and his two successors each lasted only a year before following suit. When Phra Khom finally returned home to become abbot in 1936, at the age of 34,

---

11 PSP, p. 53.

everything was in decay and much had been abandoned.[12]
He had to start again, almost from scratch.

In 1932, while Phra Khom was studying in Suphanburi, the absolute monarchy was overthrown in a bloodless
coup d'état. By the time he returned home, Rama VII had
abdicated and moved to the UK. Luang Phor Khom's early
career as an abbot thus coincided with the rise of the
strongly nationalist regime of the Khana Ratsadorn (Citizens' Party) and its campaign to encourage nationalism in
the population it controlled. His country was now entirely
in the hands of commoner politicians, civil and military.
The Citizens' Party leaders were also, to differing degrees,
committed to constitutionalism and electoral democracy
and it was thus in their interest to break the monarchy's
authoritarian domination of the Sangha. They were quite
aware that 260 of the country's *wat* were controlled by the
monarchist Thammayut sect, while 17,305 were in the
hands of the traditional, decentralized Mahanikai sect.
They also observed the appearance of an angry Young
Monks movement in 1934. Hence, in 1938, the state ap-
pointed the first Mahanikai Supreme Patriarch. In 1942,
an act was finally passed by parliament which substantially
democratized the whole structure of the Sangha—it now
had its own Ecclesiastical Assembly. (This serious reform

---

12 See ST, p. 24, and PSP, p. 52.

lasted until 1962, when dictator Sarit Thanarat, allying himself with the young monarch Rama IX, reimposed parts of the Act of 1902, brought the Thammayut monks back to power and persecuted Mahanikai monks thought to be sympathetic to 'communism'.)[13]

What seems clear is that Luang Phor Khom was a clever, disciplined and ambitious young man with strong provincial roots. In his youth, under the absolutist monarchy, when state-managed education was still in its early stages, monkhood was the only way 'up' for a farmer's son. His three impressionable years in Bangkok could have given him ideas of what a grand *wat* looked like, to be equalled and eventually surpassed by an even grander *wat* back home. By the time he became abbot, the 'old order' was, for the time being, gone and new opportunities were becoming available for the talented.

The sources at hand tell us very little about the next 21 years of Luang Phor Khom's rule but they are indicative. From the beginning of his abbotship he was an energetic builder. In 1937, a sermon hall, costing 102,500 baht—the good old pre-1997 crash variety—was completed; in 1938, schoolroom tables were purchased for teaching young monks and repairs carried out on the rotting sleeping

---

13 For an excellent analysis of these acts, their political and religious contexts and the political ideologies and interests behind them, see Tiyavanich, *Forest Recollections*, pp. 10, 187–93 and 229–39.

quarters, costing 500 baht; in 1944, 30 *rai* (48,000 square metres) of land was purchased to begin construction of an *ubosot* (central sanctuary) (no price given, so probably a donation); from 1945 to 1951, the *ubosot* was constructed with reinforced concrete, bricks, cement and teak, costing 345,000 baht; in 1952, the sermon hall was repaired and an additional hall built, costing 20,000 baht; in 1953, a school-house was constructed for budding Dharma scholars, costing 30,000 baht; and, in 1954, a concrete road was built from the pier on the canal to the sermon hall. All together, about half a million baht was spent over two decades. During the same period, he won official accreditation from the Sangha bureaucracy (1946) and a Bangkok-designated name for his *wat*, Wat Potharam (1951). (But the locals continued to call it Wat Phai Rong Wua and, after Luang Phor Khom's death 40 years later, the Sangha yielded and approved the locals' term as the official name.)[14]

What lay behind this early building programme? Sanoh Thianthong, writing about Luang Phor Khom's educational qualifications, adds that the young abbot of the 1930s was good at the abacus and calculations as well as skilled as a painter-draughtsman, carpenter and builder (architect?). Luang Phor Khom himself later described the religious importance of these skills:

---

14 ST, pp. 126–7; PSP, p. 54.

In the future, if there are no longer any *wat* then Buddhism will not survive. The Buddha's words will exist only on paper and will no longer spread into the people's hearts. The material constructions erected by devout Buddhists, such as ordainment halls, sanctuaries, stupas and Buddha images, proclaim the truth of the Buddhist religion. These days, monks are weak and disheartened. They have no perseverance. If they were forced to live on barren soil or in the jungle, there would be no more new monks.[15]

But it is significant that he also said: 'We do all this, in one sense, because if we are tired from work then we will not be disturbed by [sexual] desire.'[16] Finally, he must have been using his abacus and mathematical ability to find ways to finance his constructions; half a million baht in those days was unlikely to have come from the poor farmers of his village and its neighbours. None of the written sources give the reader a clear picture of how Luang Phor Khom raised money.[17] It seems, however, that it was in this period that he got into the business of amulet-making on a substantial scale. According to him:

---

15 PSP, pp. 54, 55.

16 Ibid., p. 55.

17 Compare the figure with Rama VI's 5-million-baht donation for the construction of the Ananta Samakhom Throne Hall.

> We wanted to construct a *wat* for the Buddhist faith but we didn't know how to find money. When we saw that people liked magical and sacred objects, we decided to enter the trade. [. . .] I made millions of Buddhist amulets, big and small. I made so many that I forget the total number. But I made them in good faith.[18]

Phramaha Suthep (Phramaha is a title conferred on a Buddhist monk who has passed the third grade in Buddhist theology) observes that many people believed in the abbot's magical powers. So they bought the amulets he produced and tried them out. The belief was that the amulets stopped bullets from leaving gun barrels.[19] This created an ever-greater demand for such amulets. It is worth remembering that early post-Second World War rural Siam was a violent and lawless place. The war itself had brought a great many guns into the country—Japanese guns abandoned after Tokyo's surrender, Allied guns dropped behind Japanese lines earlier on—and most of these fell into private hands. The Thai police force, relatively small in those days, had only a minimal presence in the remote rural areas. Furthermore, Suphanburi had long been famous for its bandits. The presence in Narokphum

---

18 PSP, p. 90.
19 Ibid.

of *praed* who once enjoyed robbery and plunder reflects the prevalent rural insecurity and shows why amulets were in high demand. Nonetheless, Luang Phor Khom recorded his religious and moral discomfort:

> When people criticize the *wat* for engaging in this business, I admit that I am doing wrong. But I remember the words of my preceptor, that everywhere there is good and bad; so even if you break the monastic code of conduct you can still keep the main tenets of Buddhism. Looking back on my involvement in the sale of sacred amulets, I am quite ashamed [. . .] Once the *wat* is completely finished, I will wash my hands of this kind of trade. When that happens I will be at peace.[20]

The written accounts are unanimous in describing 1957 as the pivotal year in the career of Luang Phor Khom, who was 55 at the time. It will be recalled that this moment was the midpoint of the current 5,000-year Buddhist era, and enormous efforts were made all over the Buddhist world to celebrate it with appropriate ceremonies and vows of recommitment. Prime Minister Field Marshal Plaek Phibunsongkhram seized the occasion to bolster his declining power by sponsoring a number of spectacular

20 Ibid., pp. 90–1.

activities.[21] For our purposes, two are especially relevant. The first was Phibun's decision to start building the Phutthamonthon (Buddhist diocese) complex in (then rural) Thonburi on a scale vaster than any existing *wat* in Bangkok. (Work on the complex came to an end when, for the time being, he had to flee the country the following year in the wake of Sarit's *coup d'état*). Furthermore, there was a spectacular rise in the government's spending on

---

21 This programme had an instructive antecedent. According to an excellent, as yet unpublished, research paper by Lawrence Chua ('Revolution, Concrete and Light: The Modern Monastic Architecture of Wat Phra Sri Maharat and Suan Mokkh'), in 1940–1 Field Marshal Plaek Phibunsongkhram, assisted by Luang Wichit Watthakan, arranged the construction in Bang Khen of a remarkable and vast new *wat* intended to reflect the aspirations of the 'Thai nation' for modernity, democracy and international recognition. Originally it was to be called Wat Prachathipatai (Temple of Democracy) but, once some serious Buddha relics had been acquired, the official name was changed to Wat Phra Sri Maharat. This complex, shrunk now to insignificance for its implicit rejection of the monarchy, had some striking features. It resolutely banished any of the royalist insignia and ornamentation that Sangkharat (Patriarch of the Sangha) Prince Wijarayan had long insisted on in order to subordinate Thai Buddhism to the monarchy. It broke with the tradition that no bones, not even royal ones, could be housed in the grand *chedi* (alternative term for a Buddhist stupa, mainly used in Thailand) where the Buddha relics were kept, by creating a sunlit mini-*chedi* with 120 niches available for the remains of people who had served or would serve the nation well. (Luang Wichit mentioned as his inspirations Westminster Abbey, the Roman Pantheon, the Panthéon of Paris and the Hohenzollern tombs at Charlottenburg!) Finally, it was the first *wat* built primarily with ferro-concrete, a modern material hitherto used only for secular public

the restoration of existing *wats*.[22] The second was Phibun's arranging a state visit by the devoutly Buddhist Burmese prime minister, U Nu, who went so far as to apologize for the destruction of the old capital of Ayutthaya by Burmese armies in 1767 and to pray for the souls of those who died as a result.

With all these widely publicized state-supported Buddhist activities, it is easy to understand why, in that magic year, Luang Phor Khom started planning and designing what he wanted to be the biggest Buddha image in the world, eventually 14 metres high, weighing 50 tonnes, on a 2.6-metre-high pedestal. This took him 12 years to accomplish, not without setbacks along the way. A Japanese lady visiting Wat Phai Rong Wua in 1966 warned him that his existing design, when executed, would still be smaller than the great bronze Buddha in Nara. Alarmed, the abbot

---

buildings and domestically produced by the crown's Siam Cement Company. The government hoped that this national *wat* would be inhabited patriotically by monks of both the big sects (the Thammayut—enjoying royal favour—and the traditional Mahanikai); but, as soon as political conditions permitted, the Thammayut decamped. The first person to be ordained there was the highly respected 1932 coup leader and ex-prime minister, Phote Phahonyothin. Note that the space of the entire complex was 50 rai, one fifth of Wat Phai Rong Wua.

22 The number of temples restored with government financing rose from 164 in 1954 to 413 in 1955 and to 1,239 in 1956. See Thak Chaloemtiarana, *Thailand: The Politics of Despotic Paternalism*, 2nd printing (Ithaca, NY: Cornell University Press, 2007), p. 6, TABLE 2.

visited Japan to check this for himself and, on his return, revised the whole structure to beat the competition.[23] It cost 10 million baht, 20 times that of all his previous projects put together.[24] Where he got the money from is unclear but it is unlikely that it came mainly from the amulets; the odds are that by this time he had created important contacts and funders in Sarit Thanarat's Bangkok.

Here seems to be the right moment to emphasize the crucial availability, since Wat Phra Sri Maharat's appearance in 1941, of reinforced concrete and cement for religious construction. If an abbot was willing to accept the concomitant coarseness of detail then he could use ferro-concrete to build, at no prohibitive cost, structures and statues on a gigantic scale. We shall recall that Luang Phor Khom's first big project, the *ubasot* (1945–51)—begun a mere four years after the completion of Wat Phra Sri Maharat—is expressly said to have been made with reinforced concrete. Was the

---

23 See PSP, p. 69, and ST, p. 132. Sanoh indicates that this was Luang Phor Khom's second trip abroad. Two years earlier, in 1964, at the age of 62, he had gone to India to visit the four sacred Buddhist sites: where the Buddha was born, where he achieved Englightenment, where he preached his first sermon and where he died. The abbot hoped to build replicas in his own country. In 1977, aged 75, he went again to India to study construction. His final trip seems to have been a journey to Burma in 1979 to pay respects to the famous reclining Buddha in Hongsawadi and to prepare to build a replica of it in Wat Phai Rong Wua.

24 ST, p. 127.

abbot aware of his debt to the Citizens' Party? Would his
Narokphum have come into existence if he had had to rely
not on cement but on expensive wood and stone?

The Sarit dictatorship, allied with the monarchy, is
likely to have looked kindly on Luang Phor Khom's world-
beating ambition, especially since Phibun's Phutthamonthon mega-complex had been discontinued on his fall.[25]
Supporting the competition in Suphanburi would be
much cheaper than anything grand in Bangkok itself, and
the gigantic religious statue would be an apolitical symbol
of national greatness in a globalizing world. Luang Phor
Khom formulated this idea by observing: 'My intention
was to honour and to celebrate the Buddha. It was to be
commensurate with Buddhism's spread all over the world,

---

25 Lawrence Chua describes an earlier (unbuilt) *sakon* monument
planned by Luang Wichit and Phra Phromphichit, to be called Anu-
sawari Thai (Monument for the Thai)—not only an expression of pure
Thainess but also 'the most important monument in the world'. 'King
Rama VI donated 5 million to build the Ananta Samakhom Throne Hall,
but it didn't effect anything in honour of the country at all,' wrote Luang
Wichit. The monument was to be 100 metres high, built on a square
base measuring 10,000 square metres. The lowest floor would have a
balcony 5 metres wide and 80 metres long which could be an 'Economic
Museum', exhibiting 'Thailand's abundant production of valuable com-
modities'. On the next floor would be a large lobby for dining, modern
dancing and, periodically, classical dance performances. The next two
floors would house a splendid hotel while the top floor would serve as a
conference hall. What fun!

IMAGE 20 (*above*) The record-breaking Buddha statue and its surroundings at Wat Phai Rong Wua (1975).

IMAGE 21 (*following page*) A closer view of the out-of-proportion Buddha statue (1975).

where it is second to none.'[26] He also predicted that Wat Phai Rong Wua would become a major business centre for his country: 'I foresee that, in the future, the area around the *wat* will become one of the greatest centres of trade in Thailand.'[27] This analysis appears to be confirmed by the alacrity with which the young King Rama IX arrived (1 March 1969) by helicopter—the *wat* was still inaccessible by road—to inaugurate the official life of the record-breaking statue now named 'Somdet Phraputtha Khokhom'. This visit was given massive publicity in the newspapers and on the radio and television, so the *wat* itself, as well as its abbot, acquired celebrity status. Following the event, visitors began pouring in from all parts of Siam and abroad. Luang Phor Khom jubilantly 'recalled' that tens of thousands of visitors came every day, so that the government had to build a special bridge over the Ta Chin River as well as a proper road to handle the huge traffic.[28]

From then on, until the 1980s, Luang Phor Khom had no monetary problems and undertook an astonishing number of projects:[29]

---

26 PSP, p. 70.

27 Ibid., p. 56.

28 Ibid., p. 57.

29 I am greatly indebted to Kamala Tiyavanich for the explicatory commentary in the following footnotes.

1957–69: Excluding the Giant Buddha, seven projects, including a schoolhouse with state support; repairing portals and building concrete roads inside the *wat* complex; a two-storey Thai-style dormitory for the monks; a replica of the city of Kabila, where Buddha was king before his Enlightenment; and of Sarnath, where he gave his first sermon; statues of Putthaborisat and Phra Thammajakr; a bell-tower; and a Buddhist secondary school; also purchased 63 more *rai* (100,800 square metres) of land. Total cost: *c*.10.65 million baht.[30]

1969–73: An amazing 19 projects, along with the purchase of 41 *rai* (65,600 square metres) of land for 800,000 baht in 1972. The projects were—a monastic cell at the centre of an artificial island inside a large hall; two *viharas* (halls for Buddha images); a square hall with a pyramidal roof in which Buddha's footprint is embedded; a replica of Buddha's footprint in granite;

---

30 Kabila is short for Kapilavastu, said to be located in modern-day Nepal. Putthaborisat means the four original assemblies of Buddhists: male monks, female monks, male laypersons and their female counterparts. Phra Thammajakr is a Thai rendering of the Wheel of Dharma—its eight spokes symbolize the Eightfold Path. Buddha's first sermon is known as the Discourse on Setting in Motion the Wheel of Dharma.

IMAGE 22 Japanese-looking Mahayana Buddha (2006).

IMAGE 23 A building in the form of the head of Hindu deity Hanuman (2006).

Chinese, Khmer and Thai portals; a Lumphini-
wan[31] park; three decorative halls (one Khmer-
style); a Chinese *vihara* in the Mahayana style;
Narokphum; a 'palace of heaven' replicated from
India with Buddha giving his first sermon; a
palace for Buddha's mother giving birth; a
Chinese-style palace in the form of a *singto*
(lion's head); a Prasat Silpa Chada (a small or-
nate building with a cruciform ground plan and
spire modelled on the head-dress for classical
Siamese dance-dramas); another Prasat Silpa in
the shape of Hanuman's head; and a site for the
scattering of alms. Total cost: *c*.19 million baht.[32]

1974–79: Five projects—a Thai-style sermon hall
in a monastery; a *vihara* with 100 pinnacles; an

---

31 The ancient custom in Nepal for a woman about to give birth was to
to return to the home of her parents. Queen Mahamaya of Kabilavastu
was on her way to the palace of her father, ruler of the neighboring king-
dom of Koliya, when she paused for rest in Lumbini Park. There she
gave birth to Siddhartha Gautama, later the Buddha.

32 There is a curious parallel with the timing of the rise of famous
philosopher-abbot Luang Phor Butthadasa's strange modernist Suan
Mokkh complex, originally founded (over 60 *rai*, 96,000 square metres,
of land) a month before the coup of 1932. Although this abbot was more
than 20 years older than Luang Phor Khom, both started their spectacular construction careers under the Citizens' Party. The very substantial
building programme at Suan Mokkh, according to Chua, was at its
height between 1962 and 1972.

artesian well to bring water into the *wat* for the school; a statue of Buddha subjugating the evil spirit Mara; a Phra Kusantho;[33] anti-flood levees; and the purchase of a final 100 *rai* (160,000 square metres) of land (no price given). Cost: *c.*47 million baht.

1980–86: Seven projects—including a Vulture Mountain with Buddha; a 100-pinnacle pagoda; and a statue of the Boddhisatva Sri Arya Maitreya, who will replace Sakyamuni (the Buddha) when the current 5,000-year Buddhist cycle ends; a *kong* (depicting the circle of Karma); and a final pagoda. Cost: *c.*7 million baht.

The total cost of all the projects ran to 83.65 million baht.

What is plain is that the pivotal period was 1969 to 1973, the final years of the military dictatorship begun by Sarit and run after his death (from drinking) by Field Marshals Thanom and Praphat. In those years, Wat Phai Rong Wua was the site of frenzied activity, including the construction of Narokphum in 1971 for 3 million baht—thrice the price for the palace of heaven built at the same time. It was in

---

33 It is likely that this name is a Thaification of Kakusandha, one of the 28 past Buddhas.

this year that Luang Phor Khom turned 69. The number of projects was drastically reduced after 1973 (although some of them remained extremely expensive). Times were changing rapidly and our abbot was already very old.

It turned out that when Luang Phor Khom died in 1990, his *wat* had enormous debts which had hitherto been concealed.[34] His successor—a withdrawn, elderly man, the son of his elder brother—left the management of the *wat*'s finances to the temple committee, mostly manned by laity. Fairly quickly mass-produced amulets of the deceased abbot were tolerated, if not exactly advertised, to ease the *wat*'s economic difficulties. By general agreement, not only out of respect for the dead man but also for obvious financial considerations, Wat Phai Rong Wua would henceforth be preserved as a sort of monument, freezing what Luang Phor Khom had created and with no more major additions made to the complex.[35]

---

34 PSP, p. 58.

35 Ibid. Phramaha Suthep adds that, in the early 1990s, when politician Banharn Silpa-archa was rising towards the premiership of the country, and eager to spend state money in his native province, the *wat* benefited from a huge expansion of asphalt roads leading in and out of 'Banharn-buri'. Local authorities were also, after the abbot's death, thinking about the *wat* as a future tourist attraction.

Undercurrents

If one considers the vast constructions of the 1960s and 70s as a whole, it is clear that 'originality', at least in the aesthetic sense, was not much on Luang Phor Khom's mind.

A good number of the buildings were intended as copies or proportional replicas of originals in India. Traditional Hindu Brahmanic motifs are common. Khmer, Chinese and Thai stylistic conventions are clearly visible (but there is nothing from Sri Lanka). We have seen that Luang Phor Khom was trying to show visitors, local and from afar, that Buddhism is a world-class and world-stretching religion, with no reason to feel inferior to any competition—not something peculiarly Thai or attached to Thai nationalism of the mainstream sort. This outlook, which one might regard as gently De Millean ecumenical-missionary, was passed on to his followers. Consider the following dialogue in 2009 between my friend Chaisiri and a monk to be identified as Phra K:

CHAISIRI. What about the presence here of Christianity and Islam?

PHRA K. Every religion teaches us to be good. But to do good or bad is up to us. Buddhism, Christianity, Islam all help the world.

CHAISIRI. But why did you bring them into a Buddhist monastery? There seems to be no other monastery that does this.

PHRA K. In the past it was Brahmanism that people worshipped but then their enthusiasm changed, leading them to worship Buddhism, which helped to spread Buddhism.

CHAISIRI. Is there something that makes our religion better than others?

PHRA K. No. Every religion is equal. Don't think that Buddhism is better than others.

Neither the official brochure nor Luang Phor Khom's notes speak of any of the constructions as beautiful or 'more beautiful' than those in other *wat*. Size and faithful copying of originals are what seem to have mattered most.

By contrast, Narokphum, about which the written sources say very little, is the opposite in every sense: original, not too concerned with replication, exclusive, local-traditional (not even 'Thai' in the modern sense). The crucially innovative aspect of this rural hell is its aesthetic form: a sculpture garden. Up to the time of its initial construction in 1971, depictions of Narokphum were usually murals—some of high imaginative quality—painted on the *wat* walls. In such two-dimensional representations, the damned and their tormentors are not singular, isolated figures but a swirling mass engulfed in a vast, flaming landscape; and next door are other murals of the blessed *arhat* ('saint' or sage who has fully realized the Buddhist Doctrine and thus attained freedom from the cycle of suffering and rebirth) and gods in a floating world of celestial light. By the traditional rules, sinners had to be depicted naked, a state of utter abjection. In murals, everyday conservative decency could be maintained (it did not always happen) by covering women's breasts and both sexes' genitals with a flame here, someone else's limbs there, an instrument of torture yonder and so on. But these possibilities are out of the question in a sculpted hell composed of individual, three-dimensional, naked figures with a placid sunlit backdrop of shady trees, a few vendors, a pond, some trucks and cars in a parking lot and a religious billboard or two. No paradise next door.

The effect of Luang Phor Khom's innovation is a kind of anarchic, semi-sadistic eroticism. Dozens of totally naked women (only a few with large breasts) are on complete display—tortured but not on their breasts and genitals. The

IMAGE 24 (*facing page*) Female *praed* being tortured by one of Yama's agents or *phayayom* (2006).

same is true, in spades, for the males. But how and why did this garden begin? To explore these and other questions, I went to Wat Phai Rong Wua twice in early 2009: first with my old friend Prasert Jarat as well as Chaisiri (who handled and recorded our interview with Mr Suchart, probably the last surviving sculptor); and then to interview the senior monk referred to earlier as Phra K, accompanied again by Chaisiri as well as Thailand's world-class filmmaker Apichatphong Weerasethakul and respected film critic Sonthaya Sapyem.

In some ways, the most startling figures in Narokphum are two *praed,* male and female, each about 7 feet tall, with ugly, menacing faces, bodies fully covered by elaborate and expensive clothing as well as garlands along with the usual paraphernalia for the making of offerings at their feet—foxtail orchids, candles and Chinese rattle-boxes containing fortunes on bits of paper. In an interview not long before his death, their main sculptor, Prathip, told Phramaha Suthep that he had lived with Luang Phor Khom as a *dek wat* (temple boy) before he was ordained and had sculpted a number of Narokphum statues of ordinary size, modelling them on evil spirits in the comic

IMAGE 25 (*facing page*) Male praed being tortured by *phayayom* (2009). Photograph by Chaisiri Jiwarangsan.

IMAGE 26 (*following pages*) The two gigantic *praed* whose bodies are fully covered, now locally called Mother and Father Gurdian (2009). Photograph by Chaisiri Jiwarangsan.

books of the time. Luang Phor Khom asked him to stay
ordained long enough to have the seniority (experience?)
to undertake a larger-than-life pair of *praed* that the abbot
had in mind. At the time he didn't feel that he was making
something powerful and he didn't call the images by any
respectful names. But his trust in and respect for Luang
Phor Khom made him change his mind when he noticed
how many people came to seek the help of the two *praed*
who were increasingly seen as endowed with magic
power.[36]

From Suchart (now 54 years old) we learned about the
respectful names now given to the pair:

> Back then I was about 13 years old and living in
> the *wat*. I started making models. Like the Golden
> Goddess and Golden God over there. But they
> were not deities then; so I continued working on
> them. Luang Phor Khom gave the female *praed*
> the name I Luptangpong because someone had
> made her pregnant. Later on, Luang Phor Khom
> decided to move Narokphum from its first site,
> which was often flooded and full of puddles, to
> where it is now. Almost all the *praed* accepted the
> move but not I Luptangpong. So Luang Phor

---

36 PSP, pp. 88–9. Curiously enough, Phra K told us that fully clothed
praed are called *phu di* (upper class beings) and ought not be called *praed*.

Khom went over to explain to her personally that Narokphum was being moved to a better place. That was all it took to persuade her to move.

The statues steadily increased in their prestige so that people would come to be cured, even seek to touch their concrete genitals under their colourful robes. Phramaha Suthep records a case where a woman danced naked before them in the hope of getting a winning lottery number. The interesting thing is the recorded response of Luang Phor Khom. Furious with her, he said that if she could prove that she got a winning number from the *wat* then he would personally give her a million baht from the *wat* funds. Phramaha Suthep notes that, today, no one pays attention to Luang Phor Khom's dare, even though the words are inscribed on the walls of the building where his embalmed body still lies.[37] Suchart recalled even stranger things:

> There are models for our statues in the Phra Malai.[38] We didn't make them up on our own, or make mistakes in our copying. But honestly, some of the *praed* may not have really existed and could have been invented. Luang Phor Khom ordered me to make each statue differently and to make

---

37 Ibid., p. 104.

38 The Thai version of the old Buddhist tradition that the Buddha once made a compassionate descent to the bottom of hell.

sure all were naked. No *praed* should have clothes to hide their shame. Luang Phor Khom told me to make I Luptangpong a *praed* who had many husbands.[39] She was always pregnant. After she became the Golden Goddess, some young guy dared to raise her skirt and expose her huge cunt. Everyone saw it. So she went all the way to Bangkok to find his house. The culprit cried in fright as if he was going crazy. He became sick and feverish. In the end, his parents brought him to Wat Phai Rong Wua to confess. Then they took him to ask the Golden Goddess' forgiveness.

Both Phra K and Suchart (by 2009, he had become a monk too, as we shall see) emphatically agreed that all decisions on Narokphum were taken by Luang Phor Khom who usually made preliminary drawings himself and gave oral instructions for the captions.[40] Phra K said many of the sculptors were barely literate and this accounted for the various strange spellings. The abbot's basic instruction, as we know from Suchart, was that all the *praed* should be stark naked and that each should be different.

---

[39] Suchart's sizeable ego makes him claim to have been the sculptor of Father and Mother Guardian. At that time, however, he was just a child and working under the direction of Prathip.

[40] Phra K went out of his way to praise Luang Phor Khom's 'imaginativeness'.

At one point Phra Suchart even grumbled a little about the second condition, saying that he could turn out identical Buddha images very quickly while the *praed* required thought and time. It is evident that Luang Phor Khom understood that, if the they were more or less identical, the *praed* would attract as little attention as rows of identical heavenly beings. But why did the *praed* have to be so ostentatiously naked?

When we asked Suchart the reason for this, his reply was strange enough:

Some people think that *praed* should be ugly and I should make their cocks big, ugly and swollen. Sometimes I feel boisterous and want to make them really ugly with huge cocks attached to skinny bodies. But Luang Phor Khom ordered me to make them balanced, befitting their place in a scary hell. He said I should make the cocks erect and it's right to make them large. If they are made flaccid then they should be wrinkled. If anyone can dislodge a cock with a pole, he said, then I will give him 5,000 baht. So it's OK to make the cocks huge. But if a cock is too large and too erect, he continued, that's not right. If the bodies are short and their cocks are enormous, then it's not right.

We can compare this explanation with Luang Phor Khom's own vigorous self-defence:

Many people have attacked the *wat* for its public display of pornography. They think that there should not be statues of naked people here. It is shameful, they say, and makes the public look down on the *wat*. In a sense, they are right. Some newspapers even took a photo of me standing at the bottom of the Tree of Thorns,[41] as a way of shaming me before the nation. I want to defend myself by asking which brothel these reporters have come from? Weren't the girls there naked? People like to criticize the *praed* at Phai Rong Wua—who always stand immobile. But nobody criticizes those '*praed* in mosquito nets' [whores]. It is necessary to make the *praed* naked. If they were to wear clothes, they would become human beings. But if they are made to look like everyday human beings, then why make the statues at all? No one will be interested in our Narokphum if the *praed* look like ordinary people—besides, where would they get the clothes? They are suffering because of their bad karma. If we place the *praed* in the world of human beings, they must be clothed. In mural paintings the *praed* never have clothes.[42]

---

41 Narokphum features a sculpted, cactus-like tree with no leaves, on which (mostly female) *praed* are seen to be excruciatingly climbing.

42 PSP, p. 79.

IMAGE 27 Illusration from the Phra Malai. There are erotic bits and pieces but the illustration as whole shows how painted hells were highly decorated and not terribly serious. (*Courtesy: Yui*).

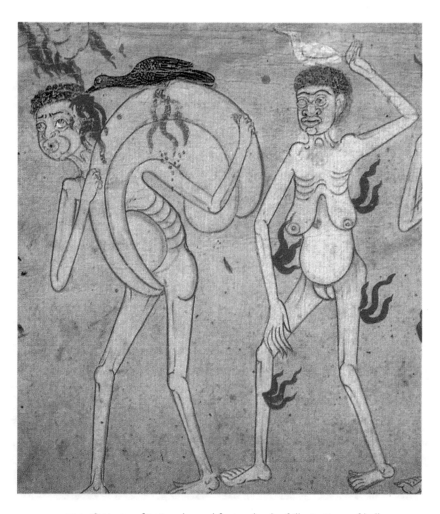

IMAGE 28 Image of tortured *praed* from a book of illustrations of hell (*c.*1780): the swollen penis of the man in front indicates the 'standard iconography' that Luang Phor Khom apparently wanted his sculptors to follow. (*Courtesy: Yui*).

Periodically, Suchart would insist that, in this matter, he carefully obeyed Luang Phor Khom's instructions: to follow the standard iconography provided by the painted (not sculpted) illustrations in the Phra Malai, which always includes naked sinners, occasionally in a comically erotic manner. But there is plenty of evidence to contradict these pieties. In the first place, Suchart positioned himself as a kind of artist whose statues required careful thought and design. He was very proud of the towering statues of the *praed* who fears no sin and his female companion who is not ashamed of sin, which took him and his wife three months to construct, while complaining that, in rural Suphanburi, it was hard to develop new ideas and images. We asked him to account for the startling change in the representation of Yama's agents over time. The early ones are of the same bodily dimensions as ordinary human males and dressed simply in country-boy loincloths. The recent ones are the opposite: males with Arnold Schwarzenegger bodies shaped by regular workouts in gyms—huge chests, flat little stomachs, tiny waists and enormous arms and legs. They are dressed in boutiquey skintight shorts and wear equally elegant boots. With their heavy, salon-trimmed moustaches and curly beards, their faces do not look 'average' Thai at all. Pressed by Chaisiri, Suchart explained that Luang Phor Khom had decided that new images had to be created since the original *phayayom* were much too

IMAGE 29 Male *praed* being tortured by *phayayom* of the earlier loincloth-wearing country-boy model (2006).

IMAGE 30 More examples of the earlier model of *phayayom* (2006).

IMAGE 31 (*following pages*) *Phayayom* of the later model: The new-age gym-rat. (2009). *Photograph by Chaisiri Jiwarangsan.*

small, dwarfed by the magical Father and Mother Guardian. So Suchart borrowed from he-man figures he'd seen in Western and Indian films and Luang Phor Khom approved of the innovation. Chaisiri observed that the head of the *praed* who liked to kill deer looked much more like the head of a foreign deer than of any native species. Suchart defended himself by saying he had tried hard to find a genuine Thai deer as a model but these deer were too scarce.

Furthermore, as Suchart indirectly conceded, it would be inconceivable to find drugdealer *praed* in the Phra Malai or those suffering for chatting up monks, telling a husband to cook rice, waiting up for a husband's return at night and so on. And then there is the curious half-ruined sculpture originally captioned 'punished for having sex inside the *wat* grounds'. The man is lying on top of the woman but with his face in her groin and hers in his behind. Neither shows any sign of torture and no cruel *phayayom* is at hand. The original caption has almost completely faded with time but someone has painted in black the Arabic numeral '69' with no mention of *praed* or the *wat*. This kind of *praed* seems unlikely to have come from the Phra Malai and strongly suggests a kind of complicity between the old abbot and the last of his sculptors. This suggestion again supports the idea of the originality of this Narokphum under the formal fabric of tradition. One might add one further indication

IMAGE 32 *Praed* of a couple 'punished for having sex in the *wat*'. The original Thai-language caption, however, has almost entirely faded but the Arabic numeral '69', painted later, is certainly noticeable (2009). *Photograph by Apichatpong Weerasetakul.*

of this relationship. While insisting that everything he created followed Luang Phor Khom's detailed instructions, Suchart told us with some amusement the story of a local teenager who had recently been caught at night masturbating on the body of a 'beautiful' female *praed*. However, the monk who spotted the lad did not punish him or report him to the abbot or to the police.

Temple Boy? Temple Slave?

How did this collusive and productive relationship come about and what could have the conditions of its possibility? During the interview, Suchart told us he had been a *dek wat* from early childhood. At 13, he had been recruited to the small pool of Luang Phor Khom's Narokphum sculptors—an improvised mix of one or two monks and several *dek wat*. This account dates the onset of his sculpting career to 1970, exactly when Luang Phor Khom's massive construction projects, including Narokphum, got under way. There seems to have been no professional training; so the group worked by trial and error on the basis of their abbot's sketches and observation of their own bodies. Over time, Suchart's raw talent became clear and, at least by his own account, he ended up as Luang Phor Khom's prime hellish artisan. How was he rewarded? Suchart said that, while he was young and single, he was content to be 'paid' with food and a place to sleep in the *wat* as well as the opportunity to accumulate merit by his labours. But, when he eventually got married and had children, his family

could not survive on this. Bitterly, he recounted that he and his wife had received 5,000 (pre-1997) baht for their three months' work on the male *praed* who doesn't fear sin and his female counterpart—amounting to about 55 baht (roughly US$2) per diem. There was not much he could do about this since the abbot said, in effect, that Suchart could take it or leave it. There was no other likely employer; only Wat Phai Rong Wua had any interest in his specialized experience and skills. The sculptor added that he had warned his older son not to follow in his tracks but to no avail; the son's wife had left him and now he, like his father, was more or less compelled to become a monk in order to survive. That in his interview Suchart unselfconsciously still described his middle-aged self as a *dek wat* seems to me indicative of a key part of the infrastructure of Luang Phor Khom's total project—unpaid, or minimally paid, 'pre-capitalist' labour. The charismatic abbot could call upon his temple boys, his monks and a pool of local farming families to work for next to nothing. Phra K recalled that the abbot never paid any wages but periodically gave tips. The official records showing that Narokphum cost 3 million baht approximately (US$300,000) are thus very difficult to believe, since the main outlay would have been simply sacks of cheap cement.

IMAGE 33 *(facing page)* Male *praed*. He did not fear sin (2006).

The old system of *kha wat* (temple slaves) is supposed to have died out towards the end of Rama V's reign but it seems plausible that it metamorphosed under modern conditions.

But from Phra K we got a different angle of vision. He clearly disapproved of, and maybe disliked, Suchart. He said that Suchart had not been born in the nearby village but had been turned over to Luang Phor Khom by dirt-poor parents who could not support him. He had eventually become a drunkard and a drug addict without taking up any regular job even after getting married. When his financial situation became worse he applied to become a monk, barely a year or so ago, but his record was such that he could only be admitted through the personal guarantee of Luang Phor Khom's nephew and successor. As long as the abbot was still alive, Suchart was evidently protected and an expanding Narokphum still needed his skills; but, as noted earlier, after the old man's death in 1990, a mountain of debts became visible and no one was interested in 'employing' Suchart since Narokphum was essentially frozen. Nonetheless, his long and intimate ties to Luang Phor Khom seem to have persuaded the successor to rescue the sculptor by ordaining him, even if there was sometimes the odour of alcohol on his breath.

Suchart unwittingly offered us another insight. When we asked him why there were no crooked politicians, gangster police and corrupt high-ranking officials in Narok-phum, he said that he had long dreamt of carving *praed* of people who embezzled *wat* monies, including dishonest monks and lay members of temple committees. (He spoke in general terms but it was plain that he was thinking of Wat Phai Rong Wua.) But this dream was impossible because he had been forbidden to try anything of the kind on the grounds that it would 'destroy' Buddhism for which Luang Phor Khom had selflessly worked for almost 70 years. It is possible that the decision to admit the pauper Suchart to the monkhood was partly designed to keep him 'inside' the *wat* rather than become a disgruntled outsider.

If one tries to put all of this information and guesswork together, it is necessary to remember that, though they were 45 years apart in age, both men came from poor families, were local boys who stayed that way and shared a rural male culture in which bandits, thugs, monks, fortune-tellers, drunkards, gamblers, farmers and *dek wat* were enmeshed. If one listens to Suchart's ventriloquizing what Luang Phor Khom had said to him, it sounds convincing—vehemence, coarseness, bad-boy humour and so on. The abbot was an educated man but educated in an idiom not alienated from rural life. It also looks as if they needed each other.

The abbot's personal museum, juxtaposing a stark human skeleton with a near-pornographic, near-naked (non-Thai) male who is anything but a *praed*, represents one form of the pictorial theme of the sexual temptation of a holy man that one finds in Hinduism as well as Buddhism and Christianity; the only difference is that here the tempter is male rather than female. David could not be part of the general imagery of Wat Phai Rong Wua. But one can be pretty sure that what drove Luang Phor Khom to acquire or order this odd sculpted David was also what drove the creation of a sculpted Narokphum where, too, skeletal forms are juxtaposed to substantial male genitals as figures for rejected desire. Perhaps this is also why these male *praed* are tortured yet their genitals are never maimed or mutilated. To build this public cousin of his private museum, the abbot needed a reliable, gifted counterpart who could help it materialize according to his instructions. It is not hard to conclude that Suchart, who is no one's fool, understood what drove Luang Phor Khom, maybe even sympathized with it, but he needed the abbot's authority and patronage. Conversely, his patron was grateful for this tact and for his spectacular statuary and so kept him under his wing. Perhaps he even told his future successor to take care of Suchart after his own death. Montaigne wrote that no man is a hero to his valet. He meant that their relationship is a dual one: intimacy at one level, steep hierarchy at another. One can see another form of this master–valet combination in Wat Phai Rong Wua.

The Future

Writing in 2002, 12 years after the abbot's death, Phramaha Suthep was not very optimistic about Wat Phai Rong Wua's long-term future. Luang Phor Khom's nephew and successor is described as a weak, reclusive man uninterested in administration and concerned not to 'develop' the *wat* but to preserve his uncle's legacy. He saw monastic discipline as deteriorating not only due to the absence of a strong hand but also because of the pressure of 'tourism'. Many senior monks no longer read the sacred texts, preferring tourism-related activities. Monks take their cellphones with them on their early rounds and, when the signal comes, lie to the faithful by insisting that it is just a wake-up call. The practice of accepting cash (instead of food) in begging bowls—strongly prohibited in Luang Phor Khom's time—is rife. The abbot closes his eyes to vendors selling alcoholic drinks on temple grounds. Factionalism among monks has been exacerbated by their differing ties to a crony-ridden, business-dominated temple committee. Relations with nearby villagers have been harmed by the committee's ruthless operations.[43] The intrusion of tourism—with the accompanying hubbub of buses, cars and motorcycles, vendors' spiels and the harangues of guides—is a source of irritation to monks who have a serious religious vocation and wish for a quiet atmosphere conducive to meditation. Other monks are engulfed in the promotion and sale of amulets, including popular ones of Luang Phor Khom's likeness, and managing the profitable cult of the powerful Father and Mother Guardian. The vast size of the *wat*'s domain means a general absence of security; after dark, the complex is plagued by thieves, drugdealers, hustlers and sex-minded teenagers who have little or no respect for the (mere) 42 monks who Phra K said were now in residence.

When we enquired about types of 'visitors', Phra K gave us the names of prime ministers or their representatives going back to the late 1980s—the very last years of Luang Phor Khom's life: Chatchai Choonhawan, Chuan Leekpai, Banharn Silpa-archa, Thaksin Shinawat, Samak Sintorowet and Aphisit Wejjawira. All came in their private capacity to avoid problems of protocol. In the same way, he said, the crown prince used to visit as a proxy for his father, but usually spent his time at Narokphum. Banharn was described as a close friend of the abbot: he often came to the *wat* to visit his political constituents and was responsible for budgetary allocations which helped build the network of good

---

43 PSP, pp. 79, 88, 101–7.

roads that ended the Wat Phai Rong Wua's early isolation. (We can be sure that Banharn's interest was to secure the political support of an influential, charismatic abbot but one does not get the impression that Luang Phor Khom was much interested in politics. He wanted Wat Phai Rong Wua to be easily accessible by the citizenry, in the manner of Japan's Nara and Burma's Shwedagon.) Phra K emphasized the missionary aspect of Luang Phor Khom's promotion of his *wat* by pointing to the large groups of schoolchildren brought in by their teachers. Narokphum could be said to be a kind of 'visual aid'—not for the youngsters' amusement but for their training in Buddhist morality. In this way, at least part of the time, visitors to the *wat* were taken to belong to the category of 'pilgrim' as opposed to that of 'tourist'.

But Luang Phor Khom's death meant an end to any serious resistance to forces which, if the *Bangkok Post* is to be believed, have, over the past decade, reduced the total number of ordained adult males from six million to one and a half. Youngsters who have grown up with violent videogames, as well as horror films and soft-porn TV melo-dramas, are not likely to be terrified by Narokphum's rustic imagery. The same Suchart, who was proud to claim (and the claim was more or less accepted even by Phra K) that Narokphum, and not the tallest Buddha in the world, was the chief magnet attracting visitors to Wat Phai Rong Wua, also readily admitted that the draw was partly erotic, with particularly teenagers giggling and hooting over the cornucopia of genitalia. Still, during my most recent visit to the *wat*, I noticed that a number of statues now had bits of cloth wrapped about their waists—thus jettisoning the theology of abjection which underpinned Luang Phor Khom's original conceptions. David's body is today covered with bronze paint, and he now wears a modest pair of shorts. A number of elaborate statue groups have also disappeared, surely because they have come to be seen as pornographic. One of these showed a naked *praed* lying on his back on a 4-foot kind of altar, surrounded by several grim gym-rat *phayayom*. His legs hang over one end of the altar, thereby confronting the visitor with an enormous greypainted flaccid penis which is not harmed at all.

One can imagine a future in which more and more of the statues will follow Father and Mother Guardians' social climb to the status of 'upper-class *praed*', even if they never acquire the pair's occult powers. The *wat*'s aura is likely to continue to seep away, since the monks appear to have no idea where to go except to 'keep things as they were in Luang Phor Khom's time' which, obviously, is impossible. Wat Phai Rong Wua is already beginning to be regarded as an oddity.

One could actually sketch an interesting future for the *wat*—in which it would be made over as a historical museum of twentieth-century transformations in Thai

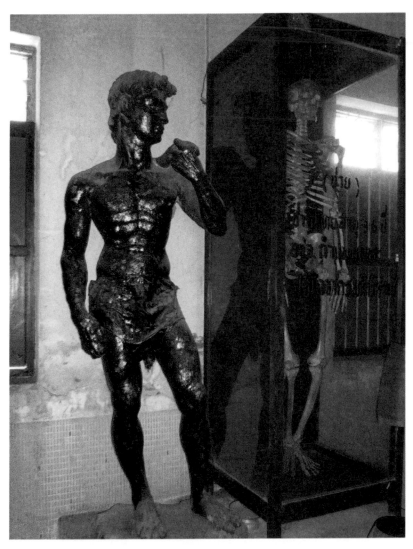

IMAGE 34 David today: bronze-painted and modest (2010). *Photograph by Yui.*

IMAGE 35 Male *praed* being tortured, without any particular sin being mentioned (2006). This statue has since been 'disappeared'.

religious institutions and conceptions. Luang Phor Khom's career, ambitions, projects and personal torment seem to me unique and, at the same time, exemplary. One could use the museum to show the sudden opportunities for 'ordinary people' after the fall of the absolutist monarchy, the rise of nationalism, the beginnings of an internationalism that inevitably accompanies nationalism, the ghostly survival in new clothes of the 'temple slaves', the mediatic pictorialization of Buddhist teachings, the commercialization of *wat* as secular and animist tourism develop, the deterioration of discipline and vocation, the impact of electoral politics and so on. In a distanced historical framing of this kind, it might even be possible to refigure Luang Phor Khom as a religious figure struggling in unusual ways to deal with his unorthodox sexuality on the eve of the triumph of a consumerist culture. But this museum is only a theoretical project so long as Wat Phai Rong Wua remains a *wat* and Luang Phor Khom is headed for a kind of spectral holiness. One only has to think of all the adjectives which cannot properly be attached to the title 'Luang Phor': ambitious, semi-feudal, frustrated, political, gay, original, superstitious, imaginative, tragic, out of date. Still, in the museum, David would have a small place denied him in the official-brochure history of Wat Phai Rong Wua.

Epilogue

During a recent visit to Japan, a good friend who knew of my interest in rural hells, gave me a copy of a Japanese book by Tsuzuki Yoichi, titled *Hell Jigoku no aruki kata* (Hells that I have Walked to, 2010). It is a kind of guide book, with numerous photos, for something like 16 hells in other monastic complexes (mostly in Central and Northern Thailand). From the look of them, almost all were built after Luang Phor Khom's original. Following the book's useful map, I set off with Siriwut Buncheun, a young Japanese-speaking Thai friend to take a look at Wat Phradeuchadom. This kitschily over-decorated *wat* is located on the outermost northeastern part of the megalopolis, an area recently taken over by old and new rich people who build weekend villas, golf courses, swimming pools and so on. Attached to the *wat* is the corpse of a Vietnam War-era helicopter, hoisted up on a high platform, with a ladder giving children access to play inside. It had been donated by a military officer who had miraculously survived a helicopter crash and who attributed the miracle to an amulet he had bought from the monks of the *wat*. Walking in the *wat* grounds, our eyes

IMAGE 36 (*above*) The corpse of a Vietnam War-era helicopter in Wat Phradeuchadom (2010).

IMAGE 37 (*following pages*) Grinning skeleton on an antique bicycle—the main attraction in Wat Phradeuchadom's hell (2010). *Photograph by Siriwut Buncheun.*

IMAGE 38 Wat Phradeuchadom: hell to the left, heaven to the right (2010).

were caught by signs on a plastered white wall indicating that one can enter hell to the left and heaven to the right. If one does not read Thai, one might easily think the directions were to ladies' and gentlemen's toilets. Hell is half underground and dark but the statues inside can be illuminated by on-and-off discoesque electric lamps. Visitors drop coins into little slot machines to ignite the lamps they wish to use. The scattered inhabitants of this hell are badly and hurriedly made, with no tags saying what sins they have committed. The main attraction is a grinning skeleton sitting on an antique bicycle.

Children popped in and out, not in the least scared, but I did not see any of them going to heaven of their own accord. These fun-fair arrangements made me appreciate for the first time Luang Phor Khom's very good decision to make his hell an aboveground, open-air and sunlit creation. He also had the intelligence to have each *praed* distinct from the other, with 'captions' painted on their bodies. He designed his hell for believers, not primarily for tourists. One can't imagine that he would have tried to create a *son et lumière* show at Wat Phai Rong Wua— performances after dark with roving spotlights, canned filmic music and, of course, tickets. But I suspect that future hells will follow the tacky example of Wat Phradeuchadom. The old man can perhaps be thought of as an ill-fated 'prophet in his own country'.

BOOK REVIEW

In Hell

MARINA WARNER

Published in the *London Review of Books* 34(17) (13 September 2012): 29. Reprinted with kind permission from the author and the *London Review of Books.*

In 1975 Benedict Anderson first visited the extensive monastery of Wat Phai Rong Wua, one of dozens in central Thailand; he returned in the 1990s and again a few years ago. Any *wat* is an imagined community, and this one, a Buddhist Disneyland, presents a special case for Anderson, whose curious book, *The Fate of Rural Hell: Asceticism and Desire in Buddhist Thailand,* enlivened with startlingly brash photographic evidence, is about currents in the national imagination, about modernity and about forms of religious practice. In the abbot's private museum, for example, next to a skeleton in a vitrine, there used to be a replica of Michelangelo's *David,* exposing himself, scarlet Y-fronts fashionably dropped, to show a sea-cucumber-like penis quite unlike the original.

Their numbers have now dwindled to a mere million or so, but 40 years ago there were many millions of monks in Siam (as Anderson often calls the country), and an abbot enjoyed—still enjoys?—the kind of prestige that Suger of St Denis or Hildegard of Bingen had in the early medieval era. Luang Phor Khom (Venerable Monk Called Khom) was ordained in 1922 and became abbot in this rural backwater in 1936; at the apex of a system of polite slavery and homosocial enclosure, he began a programme of intensive building, with funds chiefly raised by the sale of amulets. The venerable monk wanted his vast monastery to make manifest the international ecumenical character of Siam Buddhism, and he had the backing of a local grandee growing rich on new industry in the area. With the assistance of temple boys, he raised colossal replicas of Japanese buddhas and Indian stupas—one of these statues was intended to be the largest in the whole world. When a visitor informed him that the Buddha of Nara was even bigger, the abbot immediately enplaned to Japan, checked the buddha out, and came back to enlarge his version.

At Alton Towers in the 1980s (I may be misremembering) there were miniatures of the seven wonders of the world, alongside the Eiffel Tower, the Statue of Liberty and Saarinen's arch in St Louis—and very fascinating they were, intricately modelled and quite embarrassingly enticing in their newfangled dinkiness. Susan Stewart writes about the attraction of the tiny and the gigantic, the souvenir and the collection, in her book *On Longing* (1984), where she identifies the erection of colossi with the invention of a collective and the miniature with the construction of the personal. But there the resemblances between the nostalgic kitsch of contemporary theme parks and Abbot Khom's weird creation end. When Anderson returned in 2009, the abbot had been dead 19 years, and *David* was now gilded all over and covered up in ample boxer shorts.

The *wat*'s chief appeal—and the fascination of this bizarre opuscule—arose from the zone called Narokphum ('Hell'), a sculpture garden filled with 'hungry ghosts' (*praed*) with their torments garishly depicted. Each statue or group was personally commissioned by Luang Phor Khom, devised and set up over a long period as the theme-park *wat* grew and grew. Cast in cheap concrete, whitened with limewash, crudely daubed with household paint, the sinners are tormented by invisible demons; the only devils we see are the *praed* themselves, as they are disembowelled, impaled, engorged, twisted, battered, pierced. Bodily tortures such as Bosch dreamt of and monstrous physical excrescences such as disfigure Satan's minions in scenes of the Temptation of St Anthony, for example, are here represented to similar effect—the *praeds*' sufferings look horrific yet are also horribly hilarious. But laughter may be, as Freud said, a defence against horror and pain. The sins the victims have committed are inscribed on their white flesh in red letters. Many are petty and local: stealing fruit from the wat, fishing for turtles in its ponds, looking for sex in the grounds, pickpocketing, flirting with monks. Some come at a personal cost: abortions, drug addiction. The abbot seems mostly to have had the usual thing on his mind, and the crimes he punished so graphically don't stretch to higher ethics or world anxieties.

There's one significant and interesting difference from Christian eschatology. A *praed* isn't necessarily dead. In some interpretations, Anderson tells us, it's an individual who's committed minor offences, and been condemned to a particularly nasty perpetual hunger—for blood and pus—which can't be satisfied because he or she has only a pinhole for a mouth. This isn't the case, however, with the victims of the venerable abbot's fantasies. Their orifices aren't scanted, and the torments warn that trespasses will lead to suffering now, in much the same way as drug addiction soon tells. Luang Phor Khom explicitly ordered his sculptors to shame the sinners by exposing their all—hence the raucous nudity. So it might have been possible, for example, to meet a lover illicitly in the *wat* one night and return the following month to find oneself depicted and branded, bloodied and skewered, one's guts spilling out, breasts lopped off and genitals horribly swollen and luridly aflame. Narokphum is a kind of Struwwelpeter sculpture garden, filled with the dire consequences of bad behaviour come from the mind of a raging celibate.

Dante put some of his enemies in his Inferno while they were still living, but Luang Phor Khom's unfortunates are ordinary folk. The Chapman Brothers' diorama of Hell (it was burnt in the Momart fire), with its multitude of tiny role-playing figures acting the part of death-camp victims and their torturers, comes close to this Thai living hell, though the latter is life-size, clumsy and brash and without a shred of pity. Khom's temple boys likewise turned for models to Superman and Batman and other figurines, and the more recent *praed* have grown muscle-bound, hard-bodied and wasp-waisted—'gym-rats', Anderson calls them.

Ogling scenes of horror gives us peculiar pleasure, as Aristotle notes with a kind of puzzlement near the beginning of the *Poetics*, though he is setting up a distinction between art and reality, saying we like looking at nasty things—at the lowest insects and corpses—when they are represented. (His observation doesn't altogether hold, unfortunately, as hanging, drawing and quartering used to be a crowd-pleaser.) But the most fascinating effect of the hell at Wat Phai Rong Wua isn't the prurience or the laughter or the attention it inspires. The pleasure principle has led to even stranger transformations.

One of the surviving sculptor monks told Anderson how, at the abbot's orders, he'd carved a gigantic *praed* of a woman who had many husbands and was always pregnant, and given her a huge cunt. But pilgrims began trying to touch her—and it—for luck. From a horrible green and warty ghoul with a bloated lolling tongue, she became the Golden Goddess, protective deity of the *wat*, and is now garlanded and arrayed in silk and taffeta. With her Guardian God beside her, she hears the pilgrims' prayers for a cure, or success in love, or a winning ticket in the lottery. Venerable Old Khom was 'furious': the fate of his rural hell was to have become a gateway to paradise. Such are the consequences, one might warn in the abbot's own finger-wagging style, of attempting to fright people into good behaviour.

From Benedict Anderson

London Review of Books 34(18) (27 September 2012)

I would like to thank Marina Warner for her friendly, amusing and sharp-eyed review of *The Fate of Rural Hell: Asceticism and Desire in Buddhist Thailand,* my 'bizarre opuscule' (*LRB,* 13 September). I am writing only to alert readers to two misapprehensions. First, at the end of a list of the tortures inflicted on the *praed* she mentions 'breasts lopped off and genitals horribly swollen and luridly aflame'. Actually, part of the eerie eroticism of this popular, hellish collection of statues comes from the fact that breasts, penises and cunts are the only body parts which are never mutilated or disfigured. The abbot of Wat Phai Rong Wua surely had personal reasons for laying down this rule, but for local teenagers, would-be pilgrims and tourists, the allure comes from the inexplicable juxtaposition of tortures with large unharmed genitalia. This explains why male teenagers can get caught masturbating against full-breasted female *praed.* Besides, it would not be easy to find many X-rated nudes in conservative Siam's museums or public parks.

Second, it is said that 'the sinners are tormented by invisible demons.' In fact, each sinner has a very visible male torturer of his or her own. I think the misapprehension here comes from the interesting way in which the agents of the absent god of hell (Yama) are represented. The earlier agents look like wiry, barefoot Thai peasants, have the same height as the average Thai male, are clad in simple rural loincloths and have quiet, expressionless faces. Later on, the abbot decided that these old-fashioned 'demons' were not frightening enough. The new generation of agents look physically like upscale versions of the two champion wrestlers who won medals for India at the recent London Hyperolympics: warm reddish-brown skins, quite handsome faces with curly-tidy moustaches and elegant short beards, wasp waists, and whopping thighs, chests and upper arms. They wear nice boutiquey boots, skin-tight shorts, armlets and fetching headcloths. (What the sculptors got from Superman and Batman was surely models of exotic masculine fancy dress.) The facial expressions are mildly intimidating, not a patch on those of India's goondas or the grim gangsters who appear in Thai movies and on the streets of Bangkok. I described these second-generation agents as 'gym-rats', but the term, alas, is not my coinage. It is sarcastic gayspeak for narcissistic fitness freaks.

Freeville, New York

From Marina Warner

London Review of Books 34(19) (11 October 2012)

I never imagined I'd be swapping observations of genitalia with Benedict Anderson, but I am puzzled when he writes that the privates of the *praed* are 'the only body parts which are never mutilated or disfigured'. On p. 72 of *The Fate of Rural Hell*, an eighteenth-century painting showing a torture victim, with his elephantiasis-afflicted penis loaded over his shoulder, is captioned '"the standard iconography" that Luang Phor Khom [the abbot] apparently wanted his sculptors to follow'. Although my expertise is limited, the photographs of scarlet sea-urchin-like or black sea-cucumber-like organs—on the jacket and several inside—rather bear out the feeling that, in this exaggeration and grotesqueness as in much else no doubt, the monks obeyed their superior. I concede, though, that under the influence of *The Golden Legend* and such stories as the fate of St Agatha, I overdetermined the wounds inflicted on the female victims in the *wat*. I'm relieved to learn, from Benedict Anderson's amiable letter, that they suffer from different, but at least less painful, attentions on the part of young men.

London NW5